The Hive and Mulberry Tree

Written by Elspeth Graham

Illustrated by Jacqueline Pestell

Collins Educational

An Imprint of HarperCollinsPublishers

The Hive

The hive is where bees live. In the wild, the honeybee hive is often a hollow tree. Every hive has only one queen which lays all the eggs. She is the mother of the hive.

Most of the other bees, hundreds of them, are **sterile** female worker bees. Worker bees do all the work of the hive, and have **specialised** body parts.

The Honeybee

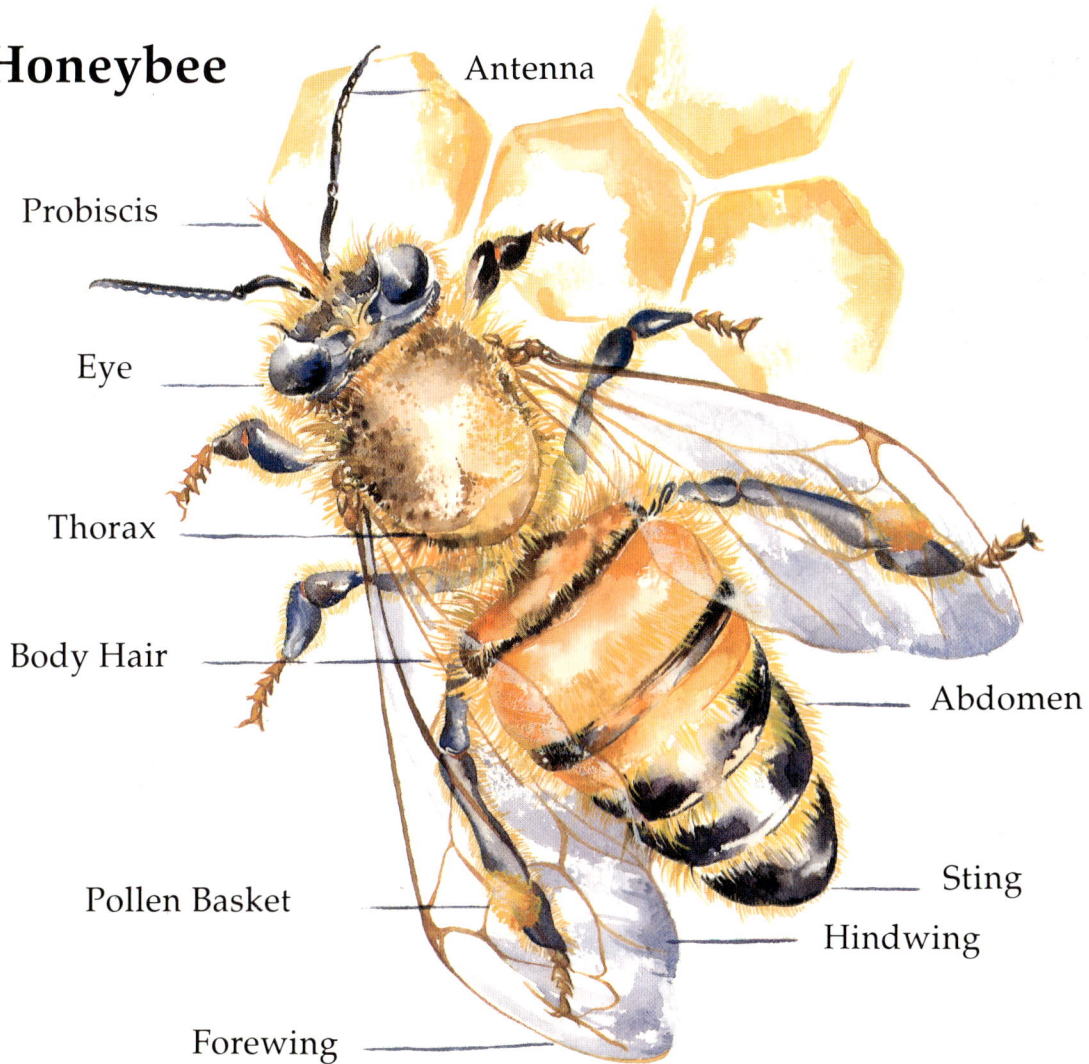

Antenna

Probiscis

Eye

Thorax

Body Hair

Pollen Basket

Forewing

Abdomen

Sting

Hindwing

Outside the hive, the worker bee's main job is gathering the nectar and pollen from flowers for food. She collects the sugary nectar with her long tongue (proboscis) and stores it in her **honey stomach**. While she is doing this, the pollen from the flower sticks to the tiny hairs on her body. Before she flies off to another flower she brushes the pollen into her pollen basket using her legs.

As she goes about her work, the bee carries pollen from one flower to another. This mixing up of pollens is called **pollination**. Most plants need **pollination** to grow their seeds.

When the worker bee which has been collecting nectar returns to the hive, she **regurgitates** the nectar from her **honey stomach**. Workers inside the hive take it in their mouths where a chemical reaction takes place to **ripen** it into honey.

In winter, honey is the bees' food supply when there is no pollen to eat. They store it in the cells of the **honeycomb** and seal each cell with wax.

6

Worker bees produce the wax from special **glands** on their bodies. They shape the wax into six-sided cells to make the **honeycomb**. Some of these cells are used for storing honey. Others are where the queen's eggs hatch into larvae or grubs.

Meanwhile, other workers have plenty to do in the hive. Younger ones clean out the cells of the **honeycomb** ready for the next batch of eggs laid by the queen.

In hot weather, hundreds of workers fan their wings on the hive to keep it cool. Others are guards, ready to use their stings and jaws to fight off enemies.

People have always enjoyed the taste
of honey. For centuries, before people
had learned how to make sugar, honey
was used to sweeten food and drink.
In these early times, people
hunted for bees' nests and ate
the lot: honey, wax, grubs,
young bees – everything.

Eventually, our **ancestors** learned how to **domesticate** bees by keeping beehives close to their homes. They also learned how to **harvest** honey without destroying the hive. Bees are kept and honey is collected using the same methods today.

The Mulberry Tree

Mulberry tree leaves are the only leaves the silkworm moth caterpillar will eat. This kind of silkworm moth – the *bombyx mori* – originally came from China. After the flightless female moth hatches from her cocoon attached to the mulberry tree, the male moth uses his feathery **antennae** to pick up her scent. They then mate together.

Frontwing

The Silkworm Moth

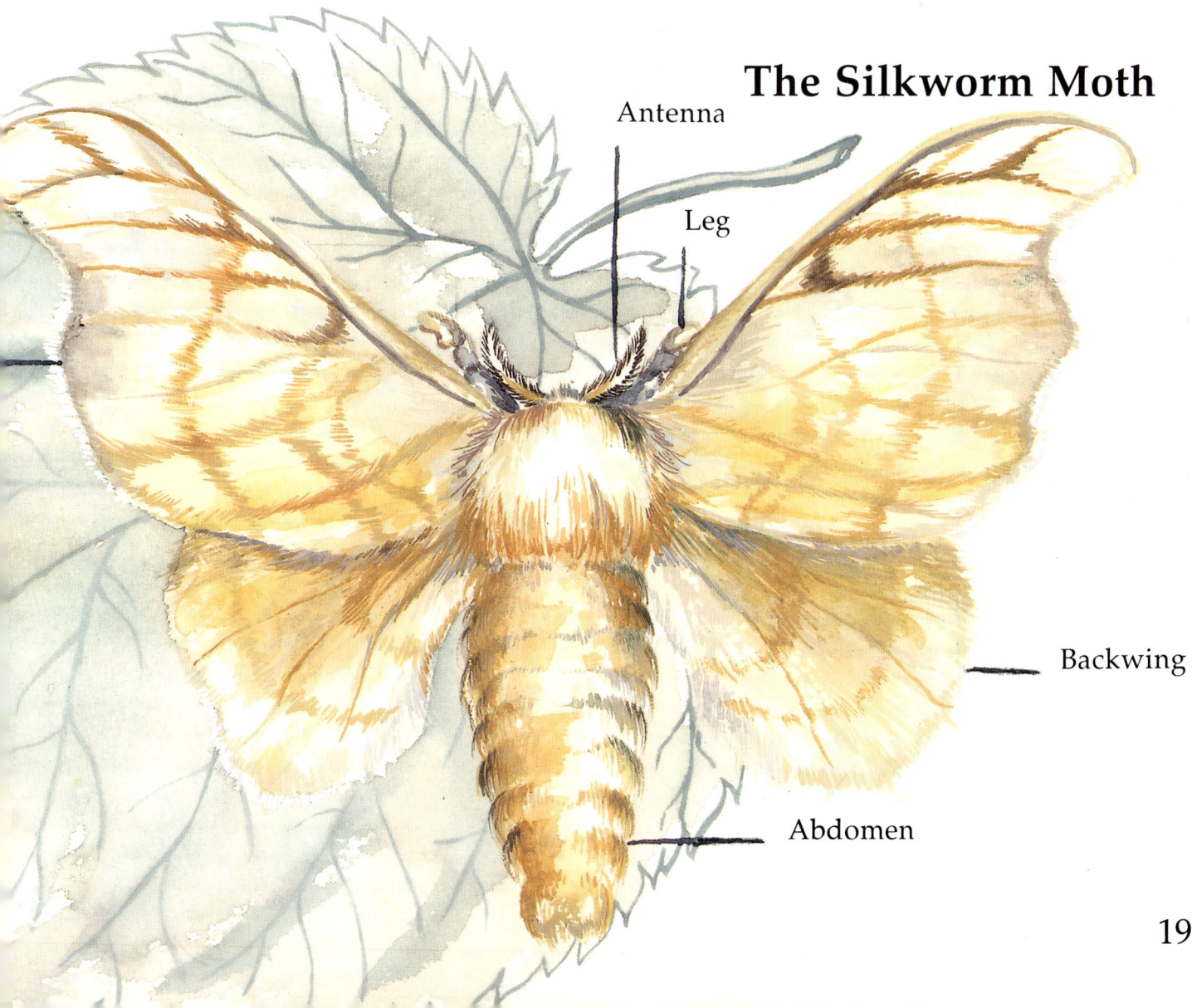

Antenna

Leg

Backwing

Abdomen

19

The female moth lays between 300 and 500 eggs. She glues them onto the cocoon she emerged from and onto the nearest leaves and twigs of the mulberry tree. If the eggs are not eaten by **predators**, the eggs will hatch into caterpillars in Spring, when the tree produces new buds. The silkworm moth lives for only a short time – no more than four weeks.

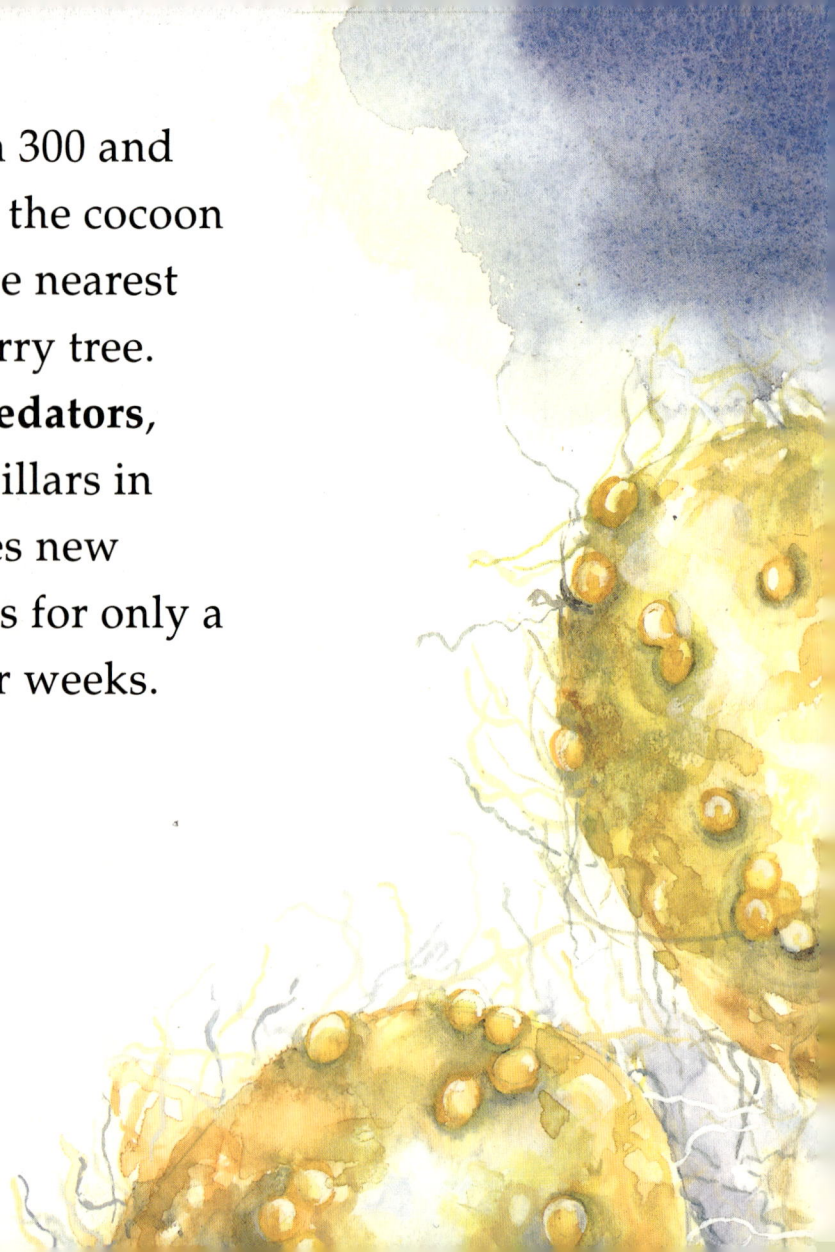

Silkworm moth caterpillars are usually
called silkworms. They are little eating
machines, and mulberry leaf is the
only thing they eat. They eat so
much and so fast that they have
to shed their old skins and
grow newer, bigger ones.
They do this four times
before they have
finished growing.

When the silkworm is fully grown and ready to change into a moth it begins to build its cocoon. It has a **gland** in its head which produces a long thread. The silkworm turns its head round and round, wrapping itself up in this long thread. A silkworm turns its head round 150,000 times to make its cocoon. On some cocoons, the thread can be two kilometres long. It's this thread that we call *silk*. All silk is now produced in factories. In a silk factory, the munching of millions of silkworms sounds like heavy rain.

The Chinese discovered silk could be used to make fabric. The legend is that the Empress Hsi Ling-Shi noticed that a cocoon unravelled when it fell into her cup of tea, so that the thread could be unwound.

Today, in factories, cocoons are dropped into hot water. This dissolves the sticky coating of the cocoon, and the thread can be wound into spools.

It takes about 3,000 cocoons to make one silk gown.

One of the properties of silk which makes it attractive to people is that it shines, gleams, and it changes colour in the light. Why is this?

Nearly all **fibres**, such as cotton or hair, are *round* in cross-section. Silk thread isn't. It's *triangular*. This means that it has three flat surfaces which can reflect light like tiny mirrors.

As silk took so long to make it was very expensive and, therefore, desirable. Because of its expense, it has been used to make the clothes of kings and queens and other rich and powerful people.

But silk isn't just beautiful. It is also very strong and long-lasting. It has been used to make parachutes and carpets, as well as wedding dresses.

Glossary

Ancestor	family member from a past generation
Antenna	feeler attached to the head of an insect
Domesticate	to keep wild animals or plants under control
Fibre	long, fine continuous thread
Gland	cell or organ which makes and keeps chemical substances
Harvest	to gather a crop
Honeycomb	storage cells made of wax
Honey stomach	a sac for storing nectar
Pollination	transfer of pollen from one flower to another for reproduction
Predator	an animal which will eat other animals or plants
Regurgitate	to bring back food from the stomach into the mouth
Ripen	to become fully developed or mature
Specialise	to develop for a special use or purpose
Sterile	unable to produce offspring

32